TRAINING MIND CREATIVE ABILITY

JOHN LOK

ISBN 979-888591827-5

Contents

Foreword

Introduction

If mind managment is the best method to train and help our learning ability and work efficiency ability to be raised. So, it brings this question: How can apply different kinds of mind managment methods to train and raise our work and learning abilities to be raised in order to help students to raise learning ability and help working people to raise efficiencies in school environment and working environment.

In my this book, I shall explain some common mind management skills, they are very simply , because we do not need to spend too much money to learn any kinds of mind management methods as well as we only spend little time to train our mind speed to be improved in our daily life very easy. I hope that my readers can learn any simply and easy mind management learning methods to train or raise your learning or/and working abilities more effectively.

Prologue

CHAPTER ONE

Daily life mind management training method

"What is the single most important skill you can learn to increase your happiness and success? I believe that training your mind will be the only important methods. Training your mind can be trained to keep health physical activities, then when you have health physical activities,e.g. keeping good life habit, then you will raise mind energy to raise learning ability or working efficiency more easier. These methods can include as below:

· How many thoughts you have in a day, you need to attempt to calculate, because if you discovered that you have too much rubblish mind to influence you need to spend extra time to decide any important matters every day. Then, you will lose time and nervous to do any important matters every day.

● Why sports people need mind management? If sports people have good mind managment, then they can concentrate enough nervous to learn how to raise their sports ability to win any sport competition more easily.

● How thoughts have energy to achieve learning or/and working efficiencies to be raised? Because if one student has good mind, then he/she can spend enough time to learn and he/she won't spend time to learn rubblish matters as well as if one working person has good min, then he/she can spend enough time to concentrate nervous to do his/her work more efficiently.

● How you are not thoughts, then you will have much chance to lose your efficiency to work when you are one working person or waste your nervous to learn rubblish knowledge when you are one student.

● How mind management needs training because you can improve your learning ability to raise your working efficiency or raise your nervous to learn.

● How Mind management can improve your personal and professional life because mind management is only the best method to help students to raise leaning ability in schools as well as working people to raise working efficiencies in offices.

I shall explain that why daily life mind management learning method will be one good raising learning ability and working efficiency method as below:

Everyone is familiar with all-out energy drain -- that exhausted day (or night) when no matter how to spend extra time to choose to watch that new movie, choose to buy which brand of fabulous shoe sale, or find whose friends to meet friendly barbecue together etc. less important lesisure activities,

What the student or the working person can be harder to recognize is a low-grade energy drain. In this case, he/she may not necessarily feel the classic signs of exhaustion -- like achy muscles or that all-over tired feeling. What the student or the working person does experience is an increasing lack of get-up-and-go for many of the activities that the learner or the working person used to love.

I shall suggest some physical activities to raise mind management energy method as below:

(1) Keeping health diet

Eating a balanced diet can help ensure your vitamin and mineral needs are met. But if you still find yourself eat much rubblish food, you could have a slight magnesium deficiency.

Some health diet professionals indicate that "This mineral is needed for more than 300 biochemical reactions in the body, including breaking down glucose into energy," They says. "So when levels are even a little low, energy can drop."

In a study done at the Department of Agriculture's Human Nutrition Research Center in Grand Forks, N.D., women with magnesium deficiencies had higher heart rates and required more oxygen to do physical tasks than they did after their magnesium levels were restored. In essence, their bodies were working harder which, over time. They also recommended daily intake of magnesium is around 300 milligrams for women and 350 milligrams for men. To make sure you're getting enough, they suggests:

· Add a handful of almonds, hazelnuts or cashews to your daily diet.

· Increase your intake of whole grains, particularly bran cereal.

· Eat more fish, especially halibut.

So, health diet professionals believe that it has close relationship to influence student learning ability and working person work efficiency between health diet and physical mind management skill.

(2) Walk Around the Block

While it may seem as if moving about when you feel exhausted is the quickest route to feeling more exhausted, the opposite is true. Experts say that increasing physical activity -- particularly walking -- increases energy. Then, walking life habit will raise your learning ability and improving working efficiencies effectively.

"I like walking because it's accessible, easy to do, doesn't need training or equipment and you can do it anywhere," says Rita Redberg, MD, science advisor to the American Heart Association's "Choose To Move" program. In experiments conducted by Robert Thayer, PhD, at California State University, a brisk 10-minute walk not only increased energy, but the effects lasted up to two hours. And when the daily 10-minute walks continued for three weeks, overall energy levels and mood were lifted. So, spending some extra time life day walking activity , it can raise your nervous to learn anythings or improve efficiency to do anythings more effectively. Time management to do walking activities daily , it can help any students and working people to concentrate on doing any tasks or learning any new knowledge more easily.

(3) Take a Power Nap

Research has shown that both information overload and pushing our brains too hard can zap energy. But studies by the National Institutes of Mental Health found that a 60-minute "power nap" can not only

reverse the mind-numbing effects of information overload, it may also help us to better retain what we have learned. So, we ought need have suitable time to nap in order to raise our learning ability more effectively every day.

(4) Reduce Stress and Deal With Anger

One of the biggest energy zappers is stress, says psychologist Paul Baard, PhD.

"Stress is the result of anxiety, and anxiety uses up a whole lot of our energy," says Baard, a sports psychologist at Fordham University in the Bronx, N.Y.Like worry or fear, Baard says, stress can leave you mentally and physically

exhausted -- even if you've spent the day in bed. More commonly, he says, low but chronic levels of stress erode energy levels,

so over time you find yourself doing less and feeling it more.

In much the same way, unexpressed anger can give a one-two punch to your energy level. The reason: "We're expending all our energy trying to contain our angry feelings, and that can be exhausting," Baard tells WebMD.

The good news, says Baard, is that we can counter these energy killers by programming more relaxation activities into our day. While for many folks, increasing exercise burns off the chemical effects of stress and anger, others find relief in quiet pursuits: listening to music, reading a steamy romance novel, or even just talking on the phone."Whatever is relaxing for you will reduce tension and that will help increase energy," Hence, sometime to spend time to listen music or read books or watch movies, these entertainment activities can help me to reduce stress or workload effectively.

(5) Drink More Water and Less Alcohol
You may already know that it's easy to confuse signals of hunger with thirst (we think we need food when we really need water).
But did you know that thirst can also masquerade as fatigue?The solution is simple: a tall, cool glass of water. This is particularly important to boost energy after exercise,
when your body is likely to be craving fluids, Ayoob says.
Conversely, if you find yourself frequently
fatigued even after a good night's sleep, try cutting down on alcohol during the evening hours. 'While alcohol initially helps you fall asleep, it also interferes with deep sleep, so you're not getting the rest By cutting down on alcohol before bedtime, you'll get a better night's rest, which is bound to result in more energy the next day.
Eat More Whole Grains and Less Sugar .The key here is keeping blood sugar balanced so energy is constant."When you're eating a sweet food, you get a spike in blood sugar, which gives you an initial burst of energy," "But that's followed by a rapid drop in blood sugar, which in turn can leave you feeling very wiped out. Do that enough times a day, and by evening you're feeling exhausted.
"But, if you eat a lot of whole grains, which provide a slow and steady release of fuel,
your energy will be consistent and balanced, so by day's end you'll feel less tired.Hence, drinking much water and drinking less alcohol , this diet activity will influence students' learning ability and working people working efficiency effectively.

(6) Power snacking is more than just eating between meal. So, a treat that combines protein, a little fat and some fiber --
like peanut butter on a whole-wheat cracker, or some yogurt with a handful of nuts.
"The carbs offer a quick pick-me-up, the protein keeps your energy up, and the fat makes the energy last. So, we needs to eat more

foods , they have high protein, because high protein foods can raise my nervous and mind and analytic abilities to be raised effectively.

How mind management method
influences efficiency

Has it close relationship betwen being effective at work And essential traits and Skills and good mind management training method?

We need to answer these question before we investigate this answer . Are you as effective, efficient and productive as you could be?

Do you consider yourself to be effective at work? Although many of us like to think that we're 100 percent effective, the truth is that most of us have strengths and weaknesses that impact our effectiveness.

Many of us could benefit from tweaking at least a few of our skills, in order to become even more effective. For instance, perhaps you've always excelled at time management. But how much time do you put into learning new skills, or staying on top of industry trends?

Or, maybe you're adept at managing the considerable demands you face day-to-day. But, when things get really to let you feel difficulties, your communication skills start to suffer as stress levels begin to rise.

Being truly effective at work can pay off now and throughout our careers. Effective workers get exciting projects, win important clients, and are well respected by their colleagues and bosses. But how can you become more effective, and make sure that you don't miss out on these great opportunities? And what should you focus on?

We'll look at the skills you can develop in order to become more effective at work,
and we'll review strategies and resources that you can use to increase your effectiveness.

Step 1: Identify Priorities

If someone asked you what your job was truly about, would you have a good answer?

One of the most crucial steps in becoming fully effective is to know your purpose at work. After all, if you don't know what your job is there to achieve, how can you set appropriate priorities? (If you don't set priorities, you'll be
forever do any tasks efficiently and effectively and you are unable to tell the difference between what's important, and what isn't.)
To identify your job's true purpose and define what you need to achieve in your current position, perform a job analysis .
This step will help you uncover your most important objectives, so that you can start prioritizing tasks effectively.

Step 2: Adopt a Good Attitude

Effective workers have a "good attitude." But what does this really mean? People with a good attitude take the initiative whenever they can. They willingly help a colleague in need, they pick up the slack when someone is off sick, and they make sure that their work is done to the highest standards. "Good enough" is never quite good enough for them!

A good attitude at work will do more than just earn you respect: setting standards for your work and your behavior means that
you're taking responsibility for yourself. This admirable trait is hard to find in many organizations. But demonstrating ethical
decision-making and integrity could open many doors for you in the future. So, focus on adopting a good attitude at work, and make decisions that intuitively "ring true." At the very least, you'll sleep easier at night!

Step 3: Build Essential Skills

Chances are that you have a lot of competing demands on your time. One of the best ways of becoming more effective at
work is to learn how to manage your time more efficiently. Other key areas include learning how to manage stress, improving your communication skills, and taking action on career development. All of these can have a major impact on your effectiveness at work.

Step 4:Time Management/Productivity

Probably the most crucial thing that you can do to become more effective at work is to learn how to manage your time.

Without this skill, your days will feel like a frantic race, with every project, email, and phone call competing for your attention.

Start by looking at your daily schedule. Do you know how you spend your time every day? If not, the answer might surprise

you! Use an Activity Log to analyze how much time you're devoting to your various tasks, like meetings, checking email, and making phone calls. It can be an eye-opening experience to look at this objectively, especially if you discover that you're spending lots of time on tasks that don't help you meet your objectives.

Once you know how much time you're devoting to different tasks, you need to learn how to prioritize them. If you know which jobs are important, and which can be rescheduled or delegated, you'll be able to focus on the work that brings the most value.

To keep track of it all, use an organizing tool like a To-Do List or (better still) an Action Program , to make sure you

don't forget vital tasks and commitments.

Being effective at work means you use time to your advantage. Schedule your highest value work for the times of day when you're feeling the most energetic. This increases the likelihood that you'll resist distractions and enter a state of flow when working.

For example, is This a Morning Task? , helps you identify your peak energy time, so that you can schedule work accordingly; and our Are you a Procrastinator? self-test will help you deal with a serious, effectiveness-killing habit.

Step 5:Setting Goal

Goal setting is another important element in working productively. Once you've done a Job Analysis , you should have a clear

sense of what your role is all about. Use this information to set short and long-term goals. The advantage of doing this is that

your goals act as a roadmap – after all, you'll never get anywhere if you don't know where you're going! Good organization is also important for working effectively and productively. If you're disorganized, you can waste a huge amount of time just looking for lost items. So learn how to file properly, and find out how to create an effective schedule .

Step 6: Effective Communication Skills

Think about just how often we communicate every day. We make phone calls, attend meetings, write emails, give presentations, talk to customers, and so on. We can seem to spend all day communicating with the people around us. This is why good communication skills are essential, especially when your goal is to work more effectively.

Step 6 :Start by developing your active listening skills.

This means that you're making a concerted effort to really hear and understand
what other people are saying to you.Don't let yourself become distracted by what's going on around you, and don't plan out what you're going to say next,while the other person is talking. Instead, just listen to what they're saying. You may well be surprised at how much miscommunication can be avoided simply by listening actively.

Step 7: look at your writing skills .

How well do you communicate in writing? Start with your emails. Most of us write dozens of emails every day. But there are many techniques that we can use to make sure we write effective emails – ones that actually get read!For instance, always keep to one main topic when writing an email.

Putting several important topics in one message will make it difficult for your colleague to prioritize and sort the information. If you do need to bring up several different points, then number them sequentially, or split them into separate messages, with relevant subject headings.

Of course, we do a lot more writing than just email. We write through IM , we write reports , and we create presentations .
You'll be more effective in your role if you learn how to communicate better across all these media, and your boss and colleagues are bound to appreciate your skills, since they'll be the main beneficiaries!

Step 8: Finding Stress Source and solutions

A little bit of pressure can be a good thing. But when pressure exceeds your ability to cope with it effectively, your productivity goes down, and your mood suffers. You also lose your ability to make solid, rational decisions;
and excessive stress can cause health problems, both in the short and long term.
No matter what you do, you'll likely experience stress numerous times throughout your career, perhaps even on a regular basis.
This is why learning how to manage stress is a key factor in becoming more effective at work.
Try to get a good night's sleep every night, and do your best to avoid taking work home with you. It's also important to
relax when you get home in the evening.
If you're not sure what triggers your stress, keep a stress diary for a week or two. This helps you to identify the events that cause you stress, and understand the degree to which you experience it. When you're feeling calm,
you can then analyze these triggers and come up with effective strategies for managing them.

Step 9: Career Development/Learning

No matter what your field is, it's important that you keep learning and developing your skills.To begin with, carry out a Personal SWOT Analysis to identify the areas that you need to work on. In addition to the technical skills required to do your job, you also need to focus on soft skills .

These include areas such as leadership skills, problem solving techniques, emotional intelligence skills , and creative thinking . Anything you can do to enhance these skills will pay off in the workplace. Also, consider if there are any qualifications that you don't have that a reasonable person would consider

appropriate for your field. If so, could this be holding you back from an advancement or promotion? For instance, would it be useful to have a particular degree or other certification if you want to apply for a management position? Are you lacking any specific skills? In some roles, keeping up-to-date with developments in your industry helps you stay relevant. It will

help you do your job better, especially as you climb the ranks.

CHAPTER TWO

Raising Learning Ability Methods

Cognitive strategies are useful tools in assisting students with learning problems. The term "cognitive strategies" in its simplest form is the use of the mind (cognition) to solve a problem or complete a task. Cognitive strategies provide a structure for learning when a task cannot be completed through a series of steps. For example, algorithms in mathematics provide a series of steps to solve a problem. Attention to the steps results in successful completion of the problem. In contrast, reading comprehension, a complex task, is a good example of a task that does not follow a series of steps. Further explanation is provided below.

A cognitive strategy serves to support the learner as he or she develops internal procedures that enable him/her
to perform tasks that are complex (Rosenshine, 1997). Reading comprehension is an area where cognitive strategies are
important. A self-questioning strategy can help students understand what they read. Rosenshine states that the act of creating
questions does not lead directly to comprehension. Instead, students search the text and combine information as they generate questions; then they comprehend what they have read.

The use of cognitive strategies can increase the efficiency with which the learner approaches a learning task. These academic
tasks can include, but are not limited to, remembering and applying

information from course content, constructing sentences and paragraphs, editing written work, paraphrasing, and classifying information to be learned.

In a classroom where cognitive strategies are used, the teacher fulfills a pivotal role, bridging the gap between student and content/skill to be learned. This role requires an understanding of the task to be completed, as well as knowledge of an approach (or approaches) to the task that he/she can communicate to the learner.

● Content Enhancement first step ?

Impacting both the task and the learner using cognitive strategies is referred to as Content Enhancement.

1. Teachers evaluate the content they cover.

2. Teachers determine the necessary approaches to learning for student success.

3. Teachers teach with routines and instructional supports that assist students as they apply appropriate techniques and strategies.

In this way, the teacher emphasizes what the students should learn, or the "product" of learning. In addition, the teacher models the how or "process" of learning. The teaching steps may include as below:

● Content Evaluation second step?

When a teacher is comfortable with the content he/she is teaching, he/she knows which parts are the most important, the most interesting and the easiest (or hardest) to learn. The teacher evaluates the content with various questions in mind:

How important is this information to my students?

Is any of this information irrelevant to the point I can minimize or exclude it?

How will my students use this information beyond my classroom (in general education classrooms, college and/or career settings, etc.) ?

What parts of this information do I think my students will grasp quickly?

What parts of this information do I think my students will need "extras" (more time, more examples, peer help, more explanation, applications, etc.)?

How should I pace the presentation?

Which evaluations are going to help me know that my students understand this information?

The more experienced the teacher is with content, the better he/she will be able to plan students' cognitive journey through the information or skills that will be unfamiliar to them.

● Determination of necessary approaches
third step

Now the teacher's attention turns to his/her knowledge of the students. Student characteristics such as intellectual
ability, interest in the subject, and general motivation to learn are considered. The teacher selects learning approaches that complement the learner characteristics while ensuring success with the content.

A teacher who teaches cognitive strategies well will connect learner and task. A strategy will be chosen because it is the best strategy for BOTH the learner's characteristics and the task and/or content that needs to be mastered.

● Routines and instructional supports fourth step

Once the best strategy or strategies have been selected, the teacher begins the work of teaching the strategy to the student(s). Explicit instruction is used to impart the components or steps of the strategy. Often the strategy will include actions or routines that are repeated each time the strategy is implemented. Additional instructional supports such as guided practice, independent practice, verbal practice, and written or oral tests may also be used.

I shall indiate A Real-Life Example to explain how above methods can help students to raise learning abilities as below:

You can compare the teaching of cognitive strategies to teaching a friend to drive in your hometown. Because you are in your hometown, you know the area, or content, very well. In addition,

the person you are teaching to drive is your friend, so you also know the learner well. This knowledge can make your
teaching more efficient, because you have two areas of expertise (the content and the learner) at your disposal. You will use a combination of explicit instructions (turn left on Church Street) and supports maps, the rule that "all avenues run North-South") to teach your friend how to navigate around town.

You may also use verbal directions as opposed to maps, depending on your friend's preferred mode of information. Just as important, you can avoid situations that could become barriers to learning (and your friendship). For example, if your friend tends to be anxious, you will NOT begin your instruction during rush hour!

● How to Select Cognitive Strategies methods to teach your students?

Because they are diverse and highly relevant to tasks, the use of cognitive strategies by teachers and students can
significantly impact important learning outcomes for students. I shall suggest some
Cognitive Strategies for Special Connections as below:

Strategy Type

(1) Orienting Strategies

Student's attention is drawn to a task through teacher input, highlighted material, and/or student self-regulation.

(2) Teacher cue to "listen carefully"Boldface type of Specific Aids for Attention

Student's attention is maintained by connecting a concrete object or other cue to the task. A special pencil cues the student to pay special attention to punctuation when he is writing sentences.

(3) Specific Aids for Problem-Solving or Memorization

Student's problem-solving is enhanced by connecting a concrete object or other cue to the task. Concrete objects are used in solving math problems.

(4) Rehearsal

Student practices (rehearses) target information through verbalization, visual study, or other means. Students practice vocabulary and definitions through games where they must orally repeat target information.

(5) Elaboration

Student expands target information by relating other information to it (ex. creating a phrase, making an analogy). Students relate the life of an ant colony to their community.

(6) Transformation

Student simplifies target information by converting difficult or unfamiliar information into more manageable information.
Procedures for protecting oneself from being burned are learned as "Stop, Drop, and Roll".

(7) Imagery*

Student transforms target information by creating meaningful visual, auditory, or kinesthetic images of the information.
Visualization of a scene described in a passage

(8) Mnemonics*

Student transforms target information by relating a cue word, phrase, or sentence to the target information.

(9) Organization

Student categorizes, sequences or otherwise organizes information for more efficient recall and use. Words in lists are placed in categories. *Imagery and Mnemonics can be considered special types of transformational strategies.

In conclusion, the use of cognitive strategies can increase the efficiency and confidence with which the learner approaches a learning task, as well as his/her ability to develop a product, retain essential information, or perform a skill. While teaching cognitive strategies requires a high degree of commitment from both the teacher and learner, the results are well worth the effort.

Intelligence methods raise
learning and remembering abilities

What is "Intelligence"? First of all, let me explain what I mean when I say the word "intelligence". To be clear, I'm not just talking about increasing the volume of facts or bits of knowledge you can accumulate,
or what is referred to as crystallized intelligence—this isn't fluency or memorization training—it's almost the opposite, actually. I'm talking about increasing your fluid intelligence, or your capacity to learn new information, retain it, then use that new knowledge as a foundation to solve the next problem,
or learn the next new skill, and so on.

Now, while working memory is not synonymous with intelligence, working memory correlates with intelligence to a large degree. In order to generate successfully intelligent output, a good working memory is pretty important. So to make the most of your intelligence, improving your working memory will help this significantly—like using
the very best and latest parts to help a machine to perform at its peak.

Thus, Anyone can increase their cognitive ability, no matter what your starting point is.
The effect can be gained by training on tasks that don't resemble the test questions. How Can I Put This Research To Practical Use For My Own Benefit?

There is a reason why the dual n-back task was so successful at increasing cognitive ability. It involves dividing your attention between competing stimuli, multimodal in fashion (one visual, one auditory).
It requires you to focus on specific details while ignoring irrelevant information, which helps to improve your working memory over time, gradually increasing your ability to multi-task the information effectively.

In addition, the stimulus was constantly switched, so there was never a "training to the test questions" phenomenon—it was always different. If you've never taken the dual n-back test, let me tell you this: I'm not surprised there was so much cognitive gain from practicing this activity.

Eventually, you will run out of cards in the deck or sounds in the array (the experiment lasted between 2 weeks to 3 weeks), so it isn't practical to think that if you want to continually increase your brain power over the course of
your lifetime, that the dual n-back alone will do the trick. Also, you'll get bored with it and stop doing it. I know I would. Not to mention the time it takes to train in this activity—we all have busy lives! So we need to think of how to simulate the same types of heavy-duty brain thrashing—using multimodal methods—that can be applied to your normal life, while still maintaining the maximum benefits, in order to get the cognitive growth.

So, taking all of this into account, I have come up with three primary elements involved in increasing your mind or brain intelligence, or cognitive ability. Like I said, it would be impractical to constantly practice the dual n-back task or variations thereof every day for the rest of your life to reap cognitive benefits. But it isn't impractical to adopt lifestyle changes that will have the same—and even greater cognitive benefits. These can be implemented every day, to get you the benefits of intense entire-brain training, and should transfer to gains in overall cognitive functioning as well.

These three primary principles are:

1. Think Creatively, e.g. finding any new knowledge that you feel that you had not mind before. Creating new synaptic
connections with every new activity you engage in. These connections build on each other, increasing your neural activity, creating more connections to build on other connections—learning is taking place. If you adopt these as fundamental guidelines, I guarantee you will be performing at your peak ability, surpassing even what you believe you are capable of—all without artificial enhancement. Best part: Science supports these principles by way of data! Teachers created not only innovative methods of creative

teaching in the classroom, but generated assessment procedures that tested the students in ways that got them to think about the problems in creative and practical ways,
as well as analytical, instead of just memorizing facts.

2. Do Things The Hard Way, attempt to do any things that you feel difficulties and you ought not feel or fear failure because fail is the success in beginning. An area of interest in recent research is neural plasticity as a factor in individual differences in intelligence. Plasticity is referring to the number of connections made between neurons, how that affects subsequent connections, and how long-lasting those connections are. Basically, it means how much new information
you are able to take in, and if you are able to retain it, making lasting changes to your brain. Constantly exposing yourself to new things helps puts your brain in a primed state for learning, which not only kicks motivation
into high gear, but it stimulates neurogenesis—the creation of new neurons—and prepares your brain for learning.

There are absolutely oodles of terrible things written and promoted on how to "train your brain" to "get smarter". When I speak of "brain training games", I'm referring to the memorization and fluency-type games, intended to increase your speed of processing, etc, such as Sudoku, that they tell you to do in your "idle time" (complete oxymoron, regarding increasing cognition). I'm going to shatter some of that stuff you've previously heard about brain training games. Here goes: They don't work. Individual brain training games don't make you smarter—they
make you more proficient at the brain training games.

Now, they do serve a purpose, but it is short-lived. The key to getting something out of those types of cognitive activities sort of relates to the first principle of seeking novelty. Once you master one of those cognitive
activities in the brain-training game, you need to move on to the next challenging activity. Now move along to the next type of challenging game. There is research that supports this logic.

A few years ago, scientist Richard Haier wanted to see if you could increase your cognitive ability by intensely training on novel mental activities for a period of several weeks. They used the video game Tetris as the novel
activity, and used people who had never played the game before as subjects (I know—can you believe they exist?!).

What they found, was that after training for several weeks on the game Tetris, the subjects experienced an increase
in cortical thickness, as well as an increase in cortical activity, as evidenced by the increase in how much glucose was used in that area of the brain. Basically, the brain used more energy during those training times, and bulked up in thickness—which means more neural connections, or new learned expertise—after this intense training. right? Here's the thing: After that initial explosion of cognitive growth, they noticed a decline in both cortical thickness, as well as the amount of glucose used during that task. The brain scans showed less brain activity during the game-playing, instead of more, as in the previous days.
Why the drop?
So, their brains got more efficient. Efficiency is not your friend when it comes to cognitive growth. In order to keep your brain making new connections and
keeping them active, you need to keep moving on to another challenging activity as soon as you reach the point of mastery
in the one you are engaging in. You want to be in a constant state of slight discomfort, struggling to barely achieve whatever it is you are trying to do.

I mentioned earlier that efficiency is not your friend if you are trying to increase your intelligence. Unfortunately, many things in life are centered on trying to make everything more efficient. This is so we can do more things, in a shorter amount of time, expending the least amount of physical and mental energy possible. However, this isn't doing your brain any favors.

Take one object of modern convenience, GPS. GPS is an amazing invention. I am one of those people GPS was invented for. My sense of direction is terrible. I get lost all the time. So when GPS came along, I was
thanking my lucky stars. But you know what? After using GPS for a short time, I found that my sense of direction was worse. If I failed to have it with me, I was even more lost than before.

Technology does a lot to make things in life easier, faster, more efficient, but sometimes our cognitive skills
can suffer as a result of these shortcuts, and hurt us in the long run. Now, before everyone starts screaming and emailing my transhumanist friends to say that I've sinned by trashing tech—that's not what I'm doing.

Look at it this way: Driving to work takes less physical energy, saves time, and it's probably more convenient and pleasant than walking. Not a big deal. But if you drove everywhere you went, or spent your life on a Segway, even to go very short distances, you aren't going to be expending any physical energy. Over time, your muscles will
atrophy, your physical state will weaken, and you'll probably gain weight. Your overall health will probably decline as a result.

Your brain needs exercise as well. If you stop using your problem-solving skills, your spatial skills, your logical skills, your cognitive skills—how do you expect your brain to stay in top shape—never mind improve? Think about
modern conveniences that are helpful, but when relied on too much, can hurt your skill in that domain. Translation software: amazing, but my multilingual skills have declined since I started using it more.

There are times when using technology is warranted and necessary. But there are times when it's better to say no to shortcuts and use your brain, as long as you can afford the luxury of time and energy. Walking to work every so often or taking the stairs instead of the elevator a few times a week is recommended to
stay in good physical shape. Don't you want your brain to be fit

as well? Lay off the GPS once in a while, and do your spatial and problem-solving skills a favor. Keep it handy, but try navigating naked first.Your brain will thank you.

3. Network, making more social network in you life, e.g. going to church, going to library , going to travelling, making frinds from internet etc. different network channel, because you can discuss any difficulties matters with other people when you need to argue as well as it can raise your analytical ability when you are arguing. So, you have much useful time to earn other people's different ideas or opinions when you need to solve any challenges every day.

When you attempt to do above behaviors every day. consequently, it can brings this result , such as :Excellent learning condition = Novel Activity—>triggers dopamine—>creates a higher motivational state—>which fuels

engagement and primes neurons—>neurogenesis can take place + increase in synaptic plasticity (increase in new neural

connections, or learning).

And that brings us to the last element to maximize your cognitive potential: Networking. What's great about this last objective is that if you are doing the other four things, you are probably already doing this as

well. If not, start. Immediately. By networking with other people—either through social media such as Facebook or Twitter, or in face-to-face

interactions—you are exposing yourself to the kinds of situations that are going to make objectives 1-2 much easier to achieve.

By exposing yourself to new people, ideas, and environments, you are opening yourself up

to new opportunities for cognitive growth. Being in the presence of other people who may be outside of your immediate field gives you opportunities to see problems from a new perspective, or offer insight in ways

that you had never thought of before. Learning is all about exposing yourself to new things and taking in that information in ways that are meaningful and unique—networking with other people is a

great way to make that happen. I'm not even going to get into the social benefits and emotional well-being that is derived
from networking as a factor here, but that is just an added perk.

CHAPTER THREE

Mind management methods to raise employee productive efficiency

Employees are at their desks for an average of about five hours every day, and companies are paying for that time.

But often the results of an employee's work vs. time spent don't exactly match up. A model employee that seems perfectly productive can turn out to be one of the worst offenders.

Accordingly, I've compiled a list of steps to help improve efficiency, engagement and productivity in the workplace.

Some of them may seem to defy logic but entrepreneurs will find that following them can lead to a happier workplace and an increased ROI.

1. Relax on Internet restrictions.

Too often, employers overly restrict the use of the Internet. This may be out of fear

that company-owned computers might be misused. However, with the amount of resources available online,

the truth is that most tasks can be completed more efficiently if employees are allowed to roam freely online in ways not anticipated by the employer.

A perfect example is the growing use of social media, which often times has a legitimate business purpose. Marketing on social media is becoming increasingly important to help businesses and employees grow, and social media can be useful in keeping up to date with competitors' latest moves. There are many employers today who simply do not allow employees to use social platforms at work.It's not always about Facebook; people can have zero productivity without even opening it. On the other hand, some employees can be super-productive social networking gurus.

2. Consistently measure overall employee activity and productivity.

In a way, measuring productivity to increase ROI is similar to sales and marketing data. In order to increase number of leads, you have to start counting those leads. If you want to increase sales, understanding the source of current sales is imperative. Breaking an entire process of working with customers in to steps, measuring every step and experimenting with improvements can lead to an increase in ROI.

The same can be said about employee-performance management. To improve the structure in general, you have
to see the entire picture -- it's even better if you can have a recorded history to compare. That way, managers can ask,"how are we doing in this May 2015 in comparison to May 2014 when we worked from different office?" Or "How many productive hours per day does the financial team have now, compared to last month when we had less on the payroll?"
In other words, in order to improve productivity stats, the reporting numbers must come first to get a clear idea what needs to be improved.

Recording usage of websites and applications can help companies keep track of productivity levels, as long as it's handled the right way. I've typically found that when employers are open about monitoring desktops, it creates a transparent, accountable environment. Managers shouldn't go into it with a lazy attitude but rather with the mindset to identify overall trends and find ways to improve productivity.

3. Set goals and use results to help employees grow.

When establishing a measurement system, managers should understand what their company's current state is and then set up rules and expectations. For example, if someone is spending five or six or seven or more hours on email and office applications, and one hour on personal sites per day,

he or she could be considered acceptably productive. Or not. It really depends on the management, which is why these guidelines need to be set within each department or the company as a whole.

Managers should have regular check-ins about goals and progress, just like any other critical KPI. For example, goals could include a 20 to 30 percent increase in sales, a least 20 percent satisfaction in support and 10 percent less time spent on entertainment websites. There should also be a plan in place for counseling employees who may be falling

behind due to unproductivity. An employee's unproductive hours may result from spending too much time on non-work related sites or too many distractions in the workplace, whether in a traditional or home office. By identifying the areas where an employee is struggling, employers can work to help the individual reach heir full potential and grow as a professional rather than letting them go (and paying the cost of turnover).

Furthermore, with certain services, employees are able to keep track of their own individual performance and hold

themselves accountable for fixing any problems. When they are able to visualize where wasted time comes from, it becomes much easier to focus on eliminating those distractions. It can also create a gamification effect of sorts – "how productive was I today, and did I beat yesterday's measurement?"

4. Calculating for brain break time.

Although understanding and monitoring employee productivity is critical to the overall health of a company,it is important for managers to acknowledge that everyone is human, and we all need a break from time to time. Short breaks (and vacations) have been proven to help the brain function better. As such, it is perfectly reasonable to allow employees some latitude in conducting personal business while on a work computer.

5. Give them a reason to believe your employees' any decisions.

Your employees are part of something bigger than themselves, but do they know it? From the first interview, potential candidates need to understand and share

in the vision of what you are doing as an organization. That vision alone will motivate and inspire your team, down to its junior members, which comes back full circle in effectively facilitating company growth.

For one company, as an example, the company's true purpose is "Improving Lives" as every team membe is aware. The team is directly improving the lives of the individuals they provide massage therapy

for, but is also improving the lives of HR teams by administrating the entire massage program fully, leaving them free to do their own jobs. Additionally, they improve the lives of CEOs and stockholders by improving employee retention and morale and decreasing worker's comp claims and health insurance cost.

And they improve the lives of people in local communities by helping businesses succeed, which improves the local economy .

6. Show you care.

Recognize every single employee's birthday. Send gifts for new babies and weddings.Be involved in employees' lives to let them feel loved and valued not only as employees, but also a family members and as human beings. "When people are loved, they will give more than you can imagine

they could for you and your cause," Wilcox says. In her company, she sends gifts to employees around every possible event in their lives. "Employees are the lifeblood of our operation. We want to make taking care of them our highest priority and to make sure they are ridiculously happy at all times."

7. Recognize the good performance to some
performance excellent employee or appreciate their performance by benefit encouragement.

When someone is doing something awesome, tell them. Recognize the individuals on your team who receive good feedback from your clients. It's important for employees to feel their efforts are being recognized, and the recognition further perpetuates their desire to go above and beyond for your clients,
which of course, sets you apart as an organization as well.

Your company may not be at a point that allows you to offer a competitive full benefits package. But you'd be surprised how far a few small (and inexpensive) benefits will go with your staff. Any companies need to give each employee a massage every month (other regional companies such as Property Solutions and Usana Health Sciences have jumped on board in offering this benefit as well). "We also provide a monthly wellness allowance our employees can use on anything health and wellness related," she says. "And we feed our team (with healthy food options) at every meeting."

8. Promote from within when some employees
performance are excellent.

When your employees see that there is room to advance their career within your organization, it speaks volumes. Find out what skills and talents the different members of your crew possess and find ways
to develop those skills for future use in your business. When you have a stellar team member, help invest in the training they need to advance as your company grows.

Promotion from within can bring on the fun. An organization that plays together stays together.Even as a smaller organization,
(Single team members can bring friends and roommates instead.)
A bounce house, live band, face painting, food and dancing prevail.

For the holidays, the company hosts a fancy dinner and movie premier night
for each employee plus one. These celebrations acknowledge to employees that the organization can't succeed without them.

In conclusion, every organization leaders and school teachers also have responsibilities to raise their students or employees' mind management training skills, instead of students or working people learn mind management skills by themselves, if they hope that every student or working person can raise working efficiencies or learning performance more effectively.

THE RELATIONSHIP BEHAVIORAL MIND AND RAISING ANALYTICAL AND LEARNING ABILITY

● What does behavioral mind mean?

Some behavioral psychologists explain behavioral mind means that in behavioral therapy, the goal is to reinforce desirable behaviors and eliminate unwanted or maladaptive ones. Behavioral therapy is rooted in the principles of behaviorism, a school of thought focused on the idea that we
learn from our environment. The techniques used in this type of treatment are based on the theories of classical conditioning and operant conditioning.

One important thing to note about the various behavioral therapies is that unlike some other types of therapy that are rooted in insight (such as psychoanalytic and humanistic therapies), behavioral therapy is action-based.
Behavioral therapists are focused on using the same learning strategies that led to the formation of unwanted behaviors. Because of this, behavioral therapy tends to be highly focused. The behavior itself is the problem and the goal is to teach clients new behaviors to minimize or eliminate the issue. Old learning led to the development of a problem and so
the idea is that new learning can fix it.

There are also three major areas that also draw on the strategies of behavioral therapy:

Cognitive-behavioral therapy relies on behavioral techniques but adds a cognitive element, focusing on the problematic thoughts that lie behind behaviors. Applied behavior analysis utilizes operant conditioning to shape and modify problematic behaviors.
Social learning theory centers on how people learn through observation. Observing others being rewarded or punished for their actions can lead to learning and behavior change.

● Does good behavioral mind influence analytical ability ?

Analytical thinking skills are critical in the work place because they help you to gather information, articulate, visualize and solve complex problems. Even with comprehensive training, there will be many times where you will be put on the spot to think analytically and the right or wrong answer could make a difference with regard to your upward mobility within the company.

You want your employees and especially your boss to trust that you will make the most well-informed and correct decisions.
Some decisions can even make or break your career. Therefore, it is of utmost importance to have well-developed analytical thinking skills. However, where do you start? Sometimes, you need to use specific techniques to get information in and out of your brain, creating highly effective maps. This crucial online course will give you the tools you need for effective mind
mapping. Read on to learn more.

● What is the different between Analytical Vs. Critical Thinking ?

Some people make the assumption that analytical thinking and critical thinking are one in the same. That is not actually true. You want to have the ability to differentiate the two so that you understand when you need to think critically and when you need to think analytically.When you think critically, you make the decision whether or not an event, an object or situation appears to be right or wrong. Once you are given information, you evaluate the data and determine how it should be best interpreted. You then make conclusions regarding your unique perception of the information. Moreover, you combine your new information with your current knowledge of the world in order to make the most accurate assessment you can make. You start to look into other pieces of data that could be relevant. In addition, critical thinking takes facts and uses them to form an opinion or a belief.

As for analytical thinking, you use it to break down a series of complex bits of information. You take thinks step-by-step to develop an overall conclusion, answer or solution. You look at something through different points of view with the objective to create a cause and an effect. To illustrate, you might try to determine why dogs wag their tails, and then come up with the scientific answer.Also, with analytical thinking, you use facts to support your conclusion and train of thought. On the other hand, critical thinking is more of an opinion-based style of thinking. Analytical skills lead you to have a more focus and stream-lined approach to solution finding where critical thinking skills can go around in circles infinitely. When you have a complex-problem or solution to find, you would use your analytical skills.

● Can improve better behavioral mind to developing analytical Skills?

If you worry that your analytical skills are not up to par, never fear. They can be developed with time and consistent practice.
Like a muscle, the more you use it, the stronger it gets. One way to start is to read more books. This may sound a little too simple
of a solution but it really works. How does it work? Well, it helps when you read as actively as possible. Instead of passively skimming over paragraphs and grazing the pages, try to look at both sides of the story. For example, if you are reading a novel, try to see
the plot from the perspective of the hero, the villain and other supporting characters. This causes your brain to think in new ways, and increase your stimulation. Thinking differently helps to expand your mind, which is critical. To expand, this powerful online
course gives you recipes to help you with fresh forms of thinking.

Another excellent option is to build your mathematical skills. Calculus, algebra and statistics all make use of logic and analysis. You need to go through each problem step-by-step in order to come up with the right answer. Sometimes, you have to work a problem multiple times before you finally figure it out. This can be frustrating, but you get better with focused practice. You can also work

through different puzzles with the goal of solving them.

Analysis and the Workplace analytical thinking So, now that you understand the purpose and how to use analytical skills,

you might not yet know how it is used at your place of work. Well, there are several ways that may not have even crossed your mind.

For instance, say you have large amounts of numerical data that you need to summarize. In this example, you might need to use the Excel

program to plot the information, in addition to Pivot Tables.If you have a large, high-level project due in a few times, you are

going to have to break it down. First, you need to look at the big picture, and ask what purpose it serves and who it benefits. Second, you need to prioritize the steps you need to take and in what order. Third, you might have to delegate several parts of the project in order to get it done on time. Fourth, you will have to manage the progress and results of the project.

● Can mind influences human behavior and health?

People who have good emotional health are aware of their thoughts, feelings, and behaviors.

They have learned healthy ways to cope with the stress and problems that are a normal part of life. They feel good about themselves and have healthy relationships.

However, many things that happen in your life can disrupt your emotional health. These can lead to strong feelings of sadness,

stress, or anxiety. Even good or wanted changes can be as stressful as unwanted changes. These family or personal matters may raise your stressful feeling, they may include:

· Being laid off from your job.

· Having a child leave or return home.

· Dealing with the death of a loved one.

· Getting divorced or married.

· Suffering an illness or an injury.
· Getting a job promotion.
· Experiencing money problems.
· Moving to a new home.
· Having or adopting a baby.

Your body responds to the way you think, feel, and act. This is one type of "mind/body connection." When you are stressed, anxious, or upset, your body reacts in a way that might tell you that something isn't right. For example, you might develop high blood pressure or a stomach ulcer after a particularly stressful event, such as the death of a loved one.

● Path to Improved Health

There are ways that you can improve your emotional health. First, try to recognize your emotions and understand why you are having them. Sorting out the causes of sadness, stress, and anxiety in your life can help you manage your emotional health.

If feelings of stress, sadness, or anxiety are causing physical problems, keeping these feelings inside can make you feel worse. It's okay to let your loved ones know when something is bothering you. However, keep in mind that your family and friends may not always be able to help you deal with your feelings appropriately. At these times, ask someone outside the situation for help. Try asking your family doctor, a counselor, or a religious advisor for advice and support to help you improve your emotional health.

However, we need to live in a balanced life. Focus on the things that you are grateful for in your life. Try not to obsess about the problems at work, school, or home that lead to negative feelings. This doesn't mean you have to pretend to be happy when you feel stressed, anxious, or upset. It's important to deal with these negative feelings, but try to focus on the positive things in your life, too. You may want to use a journal to keep track of things that make you feel happy or peaceful. Some research has shown that having a positive outlook can improve your quality of life and give your health a boost. You may also need to find ways to let go of some things in your life that make you feel stressed and overwhelmed. Make time for things you enjoy.People with resilience are able to cope with stress in a healthy way. Resilience can be learned and strengthened with different strategies. These include having social support, keeping a positive view of yourself, accepting change, and keeping things in perspective. A counselor or therapist can help you achieve this goal with cognitive behavioral therapy (CBT).

You need often to calm your mind and body.
Relaxation methods, such as meditation, listening to music, listening to guided imagery tracks, yoga, and Tai Chi are useful
ways to bring your emotions into balance. Free guided imagery videos are also available on
Meditation is a form of guided thought. It can take many forms. For example, you may do it by exercising, stretching, or breathing deeply. Ask your family doctor for advice about relaxation methods.

To have good emotional health, it's important to take care of your body by having a regular routine for eating healthy meals,
getting enough sleep, and exercising to relieve pent-up tension. Avoid overeating and don't abuse drugs or alcohol. Using drugs or alcohol just causes other issues, such as family and health problems.

● Does it have relationship between behavioral mind and analytical ability ?

Guilford's seminal studies (Guilford, 1967) propose that an average level of intelligence is required to demonstrate a creative skill. However, according to the threshold theory, in individuals with high levels of intelligence
(IQ ? 120) creativity is no longer related to intelligence. Studies that have explored this phenomenon have shown inconsistent
results. Most of the available literature has originated from Western countries find a between different measures of IQ and creativity. The goal of this study was to find a using tasks of analytical skills (verbal, scientific and mechanical reasoning) and creativity (fluency, flexibility, originality and elaboration) by conducting segmented regression analysis in a representative sample of Saudi

Arabian students.

The sample of 4368 3rd to 11th grade students (53.1% girls) was divided into three grade-groups (3rd–5th, 6th–8th, and 9th–11th). A discover was found only for 6th–8th graders at a level of analytical skills of 108.8, and at 108.4 for 9th–11th graders. The analysis of gender differences showed that the threshold was significantly higher for boys than girls in the group of 9th–11th graders (105.6 for boys, 81.46 for girls). These discoveres were generally lower than those reported in other studies. Contrary to the relationship between creativity and analytical skills was positive and significant only above the thresholds. Potential factors accounting for these findings may be the type of analytical skills tasks, more related with crystallize intelligence and the culture-specific educational experiences of Saudi children.

IN conclusion, it seems that childrens' behavioral mind performance will implies that whether their analystical abilities are high or low. Also, it can conclude that childrens' high or low analytical abilities are influenced by their daily behavioral mind performance. It means that good or correct mind can cause correct behavioral performance to them. If one child can be taught to learn to observe any things or matters in the right mind by the teacher. Then, it will be influenced to them to raise high analytical skills or abilities in possible. It explains that if the person , e.g. student can have good psychological mind to attempt to judge to do any matters or anythings, then the student ought have high level of analytical ability or skill in possible. Then, when he has better analytical ability, he will feel easy to learn or it can encourage him to raise interest to learn.

Consequently, the student can raise learning ability in order to learn any new knowledge more easily. So, training high analytical ability , it needs to depend on

how to train young people have good behavioral mind to judge anythings or matters daily. I believe that training better behavioral mind will be only the best method to raise student's analytical ability in order to let they feel easy to learn in education industry aspect.

Also, you might have to resolve a technical issue. Your first step would be to determine the cause of the problem. Then, you have to fix the error. After that, you want to take preventative measures to ensure it never happens again. All of these things require questioning, researching and analytical problem solving techniques. Without strong analytical thinking skills, you might come up with the wrong answers that could be detrimental to your workplace reputation. For more important steps, you should check out this article on analytical reasoning.